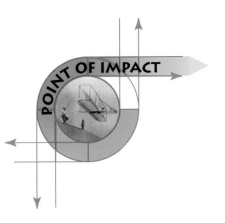

POINT OF IMPACT

Kitty Hawk

The Flight of the Wright Brothers

KAREN PRICE HOSSELL

Heinemann Library
Chicago, Illinois

© 2003 Reed Educational & Professional Publishing
Published by Heinemann Library,
an imprint of Reed Educational & Professional Publishing,
Chicago, Illinois

Customer Service 888-454-2279

Visit our website at www.heinemannlibrary.com

Designed by Roslyn Broder
Printed in the United States by Lake Book Manufacturing, Inc.

07 06 05 04 03
10 9 8 7 6 5 4 3 2 1

Library of Congress Cataloging-in-Publication Data
Price Hossell, Karen, 1957-
  Kitty Hawk : the flight of the Wright brothers / by Karen Price Hossell.
      p. cm. -- (Point of impact)
Summary: Explores the history of human flight, from the first experiments at Kitty Hawk to superjumbo jets, focusing on the contributions made by the Wright Brothers and featuring first-hand accounts of early pilots and observers.
  ISBN 1-58810-907-0 (HC), 1-40340-714-2 (Pbk)
  1. Wright, Orville, 1871-1948--Juvenile literature. 2. Wright, Wilbur, 1867-1912--Juvenile literature. 3. Aeronautics--United States--Biography--Juvenile literature. 4. Inventors--United States--Biography--Juvenile literature. 5. Aeronautics--United States--History--Juvenile literature. [1. Wright, Orville, 1871-1948. 2. Wright, Wilbur, 1867-1912. 3. Aeronautics--History. 4. Aeronautics--Biography.] I. Series.
  TL540.W7 P75 2002
  629.13'0092'273--dc21

2001008696

Acknowledgments
The author and publishers are grateful to the following for permission to reproduce copyright material:
pp. 4, 15, 16, 21 Courtesy of Special Collections & Archives, Wright State University; p. 5 AP/Wide World Photos; pp. 6, 7, 9, 10, 11, 13, 18, 19, 20 Bettmann/Corbis; pp. 8, 24, 27 Hulton-Deutsch Collection/Corbis; pp. 12, 23 Underwood & Underwood/Corbis; pp. 17, 22, 25, 26 Corbis; p. 28 Douglas C. Pizac/ AP/Wide World Photos; p. 29 Aero Graphics, Inc./Corbis.

Cover photograph by (T-B): Special Collections & Archives, Wright State University; National Aviation Museum/Corbis.

The author would like to thank her parents, her husband, David, and her editor, Angela McHaney Brown. The publisher would like to thank Mark Adamic for his comments in the preparation of this book.

Some words are shown in bold, **like this.** You can find out what they mean by looking in the glossary.

Contents

The Flight at Kitty Hawk

On December 17, 1903, two brothers stood on the wind-swept sands of Kill Devil Hill near Kitty Hawk, North Carolina. The plane they had built sat on a wooden track on the sand. The brothers, Wilbur and Orville, flipped a coin. Orville won the flip and the brothers shook hands. Then Orville climbed into the plane, lay down on his stomach, and gripped the controls. The five other men who were standing some distance away began to clap. "Let's go, Orville!" they shouted. "This is it!"

Orville's luck with a coin toss made him the first man to fly a motorized airplane.

The plane's engine started up. The **propellers** started to turn. Wilbur ran alongside the plane, holding one edge of the wing to steady the machine. After traveling about 40 feet (12 meters), the plane lifted into the air. Orville began to work the controls that kept the plane steady. But suddenly the plane dipped, and the men on the ground held their breath. Then they breathed out with relief as the plane lifted again. It sailed along for about 100 feet (30.5 meters) before landing in the sand.

Success!

The men congratulated Wilbur and Orville. One of them ran to the nearby post office. "They have done it! They have done it!" he cried. He had good reason to be excited. Orville Wright was the first man ever to fly a motorized airplane.

The Wright brothers had experimented with flight for more than four years. Every year since 1900, they had traveled from their home in Dayton, Ohio, to Kitty Hawk to test flying machines. First they flew **gliders,** trying out several types. They measured the distance and level of difficulty of each flight. This was the first year, though, that the Wright brothers had used a motor.

Wilbur and Orville Wright were not the first people to try to fly. For thousands of years, people had dreamed of flying. They made wings and jumped from rooftops. They made balloons and sailed them into the sky. But until that cool December day, no man had flown in a machine powered by an engine.

The brothers' years of hard work paid off when their airplane lifted off the sand of Kill Devil Hill. The flight was so important that it can be seen as a turning point in transportation, science and technology, warfare, and many other areas of life.

Orville and Wilbur's accomplishment was the result of many hours of study and experimentation.

Early Flight

People have always wanted to fly. History is full of stories of men jumping off towers and rooftops, flapping their arms as they fell to the ground. These men were convinced that the only reason people could not fly was because they did not have wings. So men built wings for themselves. They made them out of paper and glued feathers on them. They attached them with straps to their arms and climbed towers. Then they jumped off, sure that their wings would allow them to fly.

This illustration shows an early experiment by a man trying to fly using a parachute and wings.

Trying to fly like birds

In the year 852, a man in Spain named Arman Firman decided that he could fly using his large, roomy cape. He climbed a tower in Cordoba, Spain, and jumped off, expecting the cape to billow out so he could float or glide. Instead, he fell straight down. Luckily, he survived.

Twenty-three years later, another man in Spain, Abbas ibn-Firnas, decided to make himself some wings. He covered the wings with feathers and attached them to his body. Then he put glue all over his body and stuck more feathers to the glue. He went to a high place and jumped off. People who saw him jump say he actually flew—for a second or two. Then he fell straight to the ground and badly hurt his back.

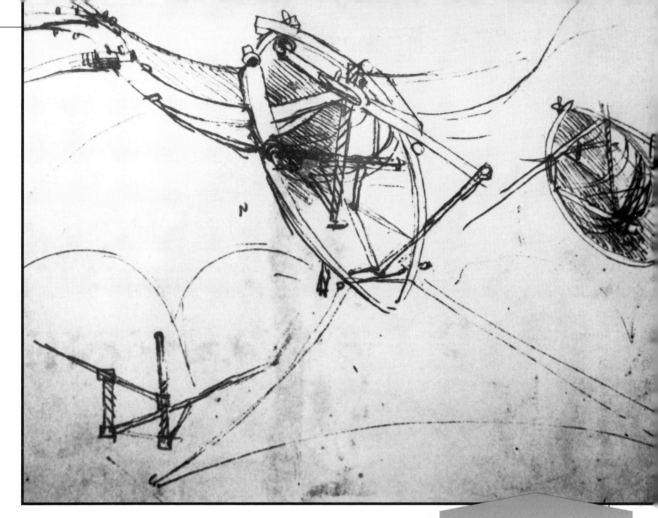

In England during the eleventh century, a **monk** named Eilmer made some bat-like wings and put them on. He climbed to the highest point in the **abbey** where he lived and jumped off. But of course, he could not fly. Instead, he fell and broke both legs.

This is one of Leonardo da Vinci's drawings of a flying machine.

A BETTER IDEA

Fortunately, by the late 1500s and early 1600s, people finally began to realize that there might be a better way to get off the ground. They began to design flying machines made of wood and fabric instead of glue and feathers. The famous artist and inventor Leonardo da Vinci drew many designs of flying machines in his notebooks. He did not actually build any of the machines he drew, though. Most of his designs had bird-like flapping wings.

Men with Wings

In 1783, two French brothers who were papermakers, Joseph and Etienne Montgolfier, experimented by making balloons. After doing some more experiments to see what materials would work best, they made a large bag out of linen and lined with paper. They filled the bag with heated air, and it rose up to 6,000 feet (1,829 meters) and floated in the air for 1 mile (1.6 kilometers), then landed. The Montgolfiers had made the first hot-air balloon.

The brothers decided to see if one of their balloons would carry people. They attached a large basket to a balloon and found two volunteers to ride in the basket. The balloon was tied down in a field. When the ropes were untied, the basket rose and drifted over the city of Paris for 25 minutes. The two volunteers had the first view of the city from the air. The one problem was that they could not steer the balloon. Instead, they just drifted along with the wind.

After Montgolfier's successful balloon flight, ballooning became a hobby for wealthy people in Europe.

Cayley's glider

An Englishman named George Cayley knew about balloons, but he wanted to make another kind of flying machine. He studied birds and made kites to study how things moved in the wind. In 1809, Cayley made a **glider** large enough for a man to sit in and had his assistant test it. In 1853, when he was 80, he made another glider. He asked his servant to sit in it and launched it from a hilltop. The glider sailed safely across a valley before landing.

Otto Lilienthal

Otto Lilienthal was born in 1848 in Germany. He opened a factory in 1880 that made steam engines and foghorns. Most of his spare time, though, was spent experimenting with flying machines. He was fascinated by the idea of flight.

In 1889, Lilienthal wrote about what he had learned in *Birdflight as the Basis of Aviation*. He built a glider and stored it in a hangar at the top of a hill. He made glides of more than 150 feet (45.7 meters) with the glider, which he would launch by running down the hill into the wind. Lilienthal also tried to figure out how to fly with flapping wings, but he could not make the wings work.

OTTO LILIENTHAL ON AIR

In his time, Otto Lilienthal was one of the few men who had flown through the air in a glider. He tried to explain to others what it felt like to be supported by air. He wrote:

"No one can realize how substantial the air is, until he feels its supporting power beneath him. It inspires confidence at once."

Lilienthal tested his gliders personally. On August 9, 1896, he fell during a test flight. He died from his injuries the next day.

The Wright Brothers

Wilbur Wright

Wilbur Wright was born on April 16, 1867, in Indiana, but his family moved to Dayton, Ohio, soon after his birth. In 1878, Wilbur's father brought home a toy made of bamboo and cork that was like a tiny helicopter. Rubber bands powered the toy. The flying toy fascinated Wilbur and his younger brother, Orville, who was born in 1871. They tried make their own flying toys, but theirs did not work very well.

For most of his life, Wilbur was self-conscious about his mouth injury and rarely smiled.

Wilbur was a good student and planned to go to college. But in March 1885, when Wilbur was eighteen, he was playing a game similar to ice hockey and was hit in the mouth by a hockey stick. The stick broke most of his teeth and cut his lips. Wilbur had to have surgery on his teeth and mouth several times to repair the damage.

After the accident, he stayed inside his house most of the time, reading and doing chores. When his mother got sick, Wilbur chose to stay home to take care of her. He did so until she died in 1889. Wilbur led a very private life up until the history-making event at Kitty Hawk.

Orville Wright

Orville Wright was born in Dayton, Ohio, on August 19, 1871. He was an energetic, curious boy, always looking for something new to do. Orville was outstanding at mathematics—he even won an award for being the best math student in the city of Dayton.

When Orville was about thirteen, he became very interested in printing, and even had his own printing press. When he was in eighth grade, Orville started a newspaper for his classmates and printed advertisements and flyers for local businesses. Orville was so interested in the printing business that he gave up his summers to work for a printer as an **apprentice.** He worked 60-hour weeks as a teenager, learning all he could about printing.

From an early age, Orville displayed a talent for building and designing.

Teamwork

When Orville was about seventeen, he decided to build a printing press. Wilbur became interested in the idea and began to help Orville. They found that they worked very well together. Wilbur and Orville looked for parts for the press around the junkyards of Dayton. The Wright brothers were successful as a team—the finished press worked well. When the press was ready, Orville began to publish a newspaper for his neighborhood called *The West Side News.* Wilbur was the editor and sometimes wrote articles.

In his last year of high school, Orville decided to go to work full-time as a printer. In 1892, though, Orville found something that was even more interesting than printing. He bought a bicycle.

Bicycles and Birds

Bicycles: The new craze

In the early 1880s, most bicycles had huge front wheels and small back wheels. In 1885, an Englishman named J.K. Starley invented what he called the safety bicycle. It had two tires of equal size and chains like the bicycles of today. In about 1890, brakes were added.

Orville Wright bought his bicycle just as they were becoming popular in the United States. Soon Wilbur bought a bicycle, too. Orville then began entering bicycle-racing events in Dayton. He and Wilbur were so excited about bicycles that they decided to give up their newspaper and the printing business and open a bicycle sales and repair shop. The shop was so successful that by 1896, the Wright Brothers started designing and making their own bicycles.

This is the bicycle shop the Wright brothers opened together in 1892.

Studying flight

Few people wanted to ride bicycles in cold, snowy Ohio winters, so business at the shop was slow that time of year. Wilbur and Orville used those days to study flying, something else that interested them. In 1894, Wilbur read several articles about Otto Lilienthal's flying adventures. As he read, Wilbur wondered whether he and Orville could make a large flying machine like the ones Lilienthal used. When Lilienthal died in 1896, Wilbur studied his final flight to see what he did wrong.

Wilbur also wrote to the Smithsonian Institute looking for books and papers on the subject of flight. The Wright brothers studied the writings of many people in order to learn as much as possible from earlier experiments. Together, they tried to figure out how to build a flying machine that could be controlled easily by the pilot. After studying how birds moved their wings when they flew, the brothers thought a wing that twisted would work best. If the pilot could twist the wing to move along with gusts of wind, he or she could control the craft.

These **glider** wings were one of Lilienthal's many attempts at flight.

BIRD WATCHING

Wilbur Wright loved watching birds soaring through the air. He studied them through binoculars and took notes on their behavior. He said the following about the bird studies he and Orville did:

We could not understand that there was anything about a bird that would enable it to fly that could not be built on a larger scale and used by man.

Kitty Hawk: 1900

One day while working in the bicycle shop, Wilbur saw a cardboard box with the opposite ends open. He watched someone in the shop twist the box as he talked. Wilbur noticed that if the man moved one end of the box one way, the opposite end went the other way. That gave him an idea for an airplane wing. He explained his idea to Orville, and together they built a kite that worked according to Wilbur's idea. They had to experiment with different wings until they got it right, but soon they were satisfied with what they had discovered. They decided to do some more experiments with **gliders.**

Choosing a location

In November of 1899, Wilbur wrote a letter to the U.S. Weather Bureau. He explained that he wanted to find a place that had steady winds of at least 15 miles (24 kilometers) an hour and wide, open spaces where they could experiment with what he called "scientific kite flying." The Weather Bureau suggested Kitty Hawk, North Carolina.

The brothers agreed that Kitty Hawk sounded promising, so Wilbur wrote to the postmistress there—Addie Tate—and her husband, William, wrote back. He confirmed what the Weather Bureau had said about Kitty Hawk, then added that he and his neighbors would be happy to have the brothers visit their town.

Located on a chain of islands called the Outer Banks, Kitty Hawk had strong, steady winds, a large expanse of soft, flat sand, and several high sand dunes.

Map showing:
MAINE, VERMONT, NEW HAMPSHIRE, NEW YORK, MASSACHUSETTS, RHODE ISLAND, CONNECTICUT, PENNSYLVANIA, New York City, NEW JERSEY, Cleveland, Philadelphia, OHIO, MARYLAND, Atlantic City, Dayton, WEST VIRGINIA, DELAWARE, Cincinnati, Richmond, Charleston, VIRGINIA, **KITTY HAWK**, Durham, Raleigh, **Wright Brothers National Memorial**, Charlotte, NORTH CAROLINA, SOUTH CAROLINA, Atlanta, GEORGIA, Atlantic Ocean, FLORIDA

N
W—E
S

0 miles 200
0 km 325

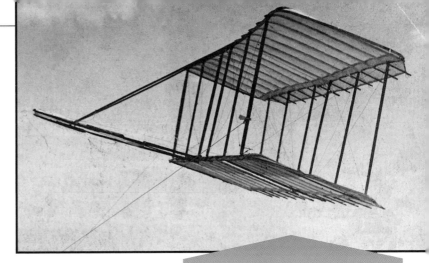

On September 13, 1900, Wilbur crossed over to Kitty Hawk from the mainland, his boat full of supplies and glider parts. For a few weeks, Wilbur stayed with the Tate family and worked on assembling the glider. Orville stayed behind to close up the bike shop.

On September 28, Orville arrived with more supplies, including a tent, food, and cots. The brothers set up their large tent on the sand about half a mile (0.8 kilometers) from the Tate's house and went to work.

When problems arose, as they often did, Wilbur and Orville worked together to find a solution.

Gliding down Kill Devil Hill

The first glider used by the Wright brothers was a **biplane** with a **wingspan** of 17.5 feet (2.3 meters). To launch it, they and an assistant, often William Tate, carried it to the top of the largest sand dune, called Kill Devil Hill. Then either Orville or Wilbur got into position on the glider. The other two men would each hold onto a wingtip and run down the dune until the glider caught the wind and lifted into the air.

The brothers tested out different wing designs by tying ropes to the glider and working it like a kite. They also put an **elevator** on the glider. The elevator was an important addition. The Wright brothers were the first to use one, and planes still use them today. The elevator moves up and down, controlling the up-and-down movement of an airplane. After the brothers completed the glider, they climbed the hill and tried it out again. This time, the brothers were able to make glides as long as 400 feet (122 meters).

On October 23, 1900, Wilbur and Orville left Kitty Hawk. As soon as they got back to Dayton, Ohio, they began planning for their next visit.

Kitty Hawk: 1901 and 1902

By July 1901, Wilbur and Orville were back in Kitty Hawk. Their new **glider** was larger than the first, with a **wingspan** of 22 feet (6.7 meters). On July 27, the brothers carried the glider to the top of Kill Devil Hill and launched it. Wilbur was the pilot that day, and he felt that the plane was not flying as expected. Wilbur made many flights that day, trying to figure out the problem.

The Wright brothers built a shed at Kitty Hawk so they would have somewhere to store their glider. They also put a kitchen and sleeping area in the shed.

When Wilbur stopped flying, the brothers took the glider apart and flew each wing separately as a kite, learning how the wings moved and why they sometimes fell to the ground. They also experimented with more twisting, or warping, of the wings. The brothers left Kitty Hawk on August 20 knowing they had to do a lot more work to learn how to control the glider.

Improving the glider

At home in Dayton, Wilbur and Orville studied the best glide they had made to see why it worked so well. To determine the best wing shape, they built a wind tunnel with a powerful fan at one end. The tunnel was 6 feet (2.7 meters) long and had a glass window on top so they could look inside. The brothers made model wings of different shapes and **camber,** or curve, and studied how the wind lifted them in the tunnel. People use computerized wind tunnels today to test models in a similar way. The Wright brothers found that cambered wings allowed the air to lift the wings better than it would lift a flat wing.

Back to Kitty Hawk

On August 28, 1902, the brothers returned to Kitty Hawk. Their new glider had a wingspan of 32 feet (9.75 meters) and a new control system. The pilot controlled the front **elevator** with a hand lever. The pilot moved his hips from side to side to control the warping of the wings. This new glider also had a tail—the first gliders had not. They were pleased with the way the glider flew, but they were puzzled by how the glider would sometimes spin out of control. On one glide, Orville tried to warp the wings, but instead of doing what he expected, the glider fell sideways into a sand dune. The dune was soft, so Orville was not hurt, but the glider was badly damaged.

Adding a tail

Wilbur and Orville repaired the glider, and by September 29 they were gliding up to 550 feet (168 meters). Still, the glider sometimes veered out of control. The brothers studied every aspect of the glider and finally decided that the tail needed to be movable. The movable tail would be like the **rudder** of a ship, allowing them to steer the glider as it sailed through the air. The next step, they decided, was to use an engine. They left Kitty Hawk on October 28, ready to spend the cold winter months in Dayton designing and building a motorized flyer.

With the tail installed, Orville's best flight was 615.5 feet (188 meters) in 21 seconds. Wilbur's was 622.5 feet (190 meters) in 26 seconds.

Kitty Hawk: 1903

Wilbur and Orville Wright had hired a man named Charlie Taylor to take care of things in the bicycle shop when they could not be there. Taylor was a mechanic, and was a great help when the brothers began to build their powered flyer. The Wrights and Taylor worked together to make an engine weighing 40 pounds (18 kilograms), which was lighter than any manufacturer had said it could be. The flyer also had wooden **propellers,** fan-like blades to help the plane move through the air.

Building the track

On September 25, 1903, the brothers went back to Kitty Hawk. They knew their new flyer was too heavy to launch in the same way they had launched the **gliders,** and the sand at Kitty Hawk was too soft for the flyer to run along the ground. They built a 60-foot (18-meter) wooden track in the sand for the flyer to run along to get to the top of Kill Devil Hill. They pulled the plane as far as the track would go, then rebuilt the track in front of the plane and up the 150-foot (45.7-meter) sand dune.

This is an illustration of the first flight using a motor. Without a pilot, the total weight of the powered flyer was 605 pounds (274.4 kilograms).

On November 28, they tested the plane's engine. It worked, but then they noticed that the propeller had a crack in it. Orville went back to Dayton so he and Charlie Taylor could fix the propeller. Orville returned to Kitty Hawk on December 11.

Hard work pays off

On December 16, Wilbur piloted the flyer. Because he was not used to the motorized flyer, though, he had trouble controlling it. He took the plane up too high. He tried to work the controls to bring the plane lower, but he was not sure exactly what to do, and the plane crashed nose-first into the sand.

When the Wright brothers tested their flyer on December 17, 1903, a few of their Kitty Hawk neighbors were there to watch. They all found themselves witnessing an important moment in the history of flight.

The brothers fixed up the flyer and moved it up the hill the next day, December 17. Now it was Orville's turn. He and Wilbur shook hands. Then Orville took his place in the machine. They had hooked the flyer to a cable to keep it in place on top of the dune. Wilbur unhooked the cable, and the flyer began to move. The wind speed at the time was 27 miles (43.5 kilometers) an hour. Wilbur ran alongside, gently touching the tip of the wing to steady the plane. The flyer lifted into the air and landed after flying 100 feet (30.5 meters).

Wilbur, who went 852 feet (260 meters) in 59 seconds, made the longest flight that day. By combining their talents for design and engineering, the Wright brothers had figured out how to build a powered aircraft and how to fly it—something no one else had ever done.

The Flights that Followed

Many of the newspapers that included news stories on the Wright brothers' December 17 flight did not report it accurately. The headline on the front page of the December 18th edition of the *Virginian-Pilot,* for example, said "Flying Machine Soars 3 Miles in Teeth of High Wind Over Sand Hills and Waves at Kitty Hawk on Carolina Coast." Part of that was correct: The plane did fly over sand hills at Kitty Hawk. But it did not go three miles, and it did not fly over waves.

Setting the record straight

The brothers became frustrated with the inaccuracy of the news stories and issued a statement on January 4, 1904. They wrote that they had not wanted to give out the details of their flight, but since many newspapers were publishing inaccurate reports, they wanted to set the record straight. They then said that they did not want to give out pictures of their flying machine—now called the *Kitty Hawk Flyer*—and they did not want to describe it in detail. They were afraid someone would steal their ideas.

Inaccurate headlines such as this one led the Wright brothers to make a formal statement about their success at Kitty Hawk.

Huffman's Prairie

Meanwhile, the brothers had already started building *Flyer II.* Instead of going back to Kitty Hawk, they looked around for a place near Dayton to fly. A man named Torrance Huffman let them use his field, called Huffman's Prairie. During the spring and summer of 1904, Orville and Wilbur built a hangar

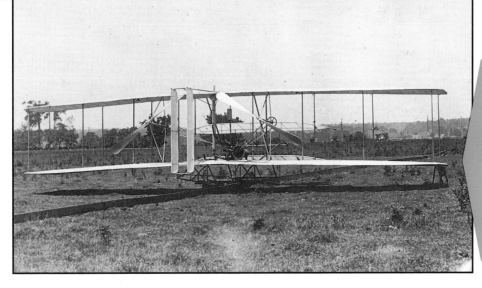

The Wright brothers built a special launching device at Huffman's Prairie that was similar to a **catapult.**

on the field and stored *Flyer II* there. On September 20, Wilbur flew the best flight to date, going 3,960 feet (1.2 kilometers) in 35.5 seconds.

Flyer III

Every time they built and tested a new flyer, the Wright brothers found ways to improve it. During the winter of 1904 to 1905, the brothers built a plane with better controls than *Flyer II*. They launched *Flyer III* in June 1905. They broke speed and distance records almost every day. On September 26, they flew just over 11 miles (17.7 kilometers) in 18 minutes and 9 seconds. By October 5, they were able to fly 24.5 miles (39.4 kilometers) in 38 minutes and 3 seconds. Few people knew about these flights, though, because the Wright brothers were still concerned about their ideas being stolen.

THE GRANDEST SIGHT

On September 20, 1904, a man named Amos Root watched the Wright brothers' flight over Huffman Prairie. In an article he wrote a few months later, he said that seeing the flight was *"one of the grandest sights, if not the grandest sight, of my life. Imagine a locomotive [train] that has left its track, and is climbing up in the air right toward you—a locomotive without any wheels, we will say, but with white wings instead."*

Into the Air Again

In 1906 and 1907, Wilbur and Orville Wright designed and built airplanes and tried to get contracts from the U.S. Army and the French Army to build planes for them. They were still not flying planes during this time, but others were.

In 1906, a Brazilian named Albert Santos-Dumont made a 722-foot (220-meter) flight near Paris. In France in January 1908, Henry Farman became the first European to fly 0.6 miles (1 kilometer). Also in 1908, a man named Glenn Curtiss became the first U.S. pilot to fly 0.6 miles (1 kilometer). The Wright brothers soon agreed it was time to go back to flying.

This photograph was taken of Wilbur Wright during one of his flights over France in 1909.

At the beginning of the year, they got two important contracts—one from the U.S. Army to build a plane, and one from the French Army. Later in the year, the brothers realized that to complete the work they planned to do, they had to separate. Orville would stay in Ohio and build the plane the U.S. Army had requested, and Wilbur would go to France and fly. The Wright brothers' knowledge of flight far exceeded that of the pilots who were being hailed in France as heroes. It was time for Orville and Wilbur to stop keeping secrets.

Wilbur flies in France

On August 8, 1908, Wilbur flew his plane at Le Mans racetrack near Paris. There were 26 adults and several children as witnesses when Wilbur took off, **banked,** rolled, and landed safely. Soon, Wilbur's flights were known all over the world.

Orville and the army plane

On September 3, Orville flew the plane for the U.S. Army. He flew around the test field one-and-a-half times. When he landed, the crowd went wild, cheering and crying. But on September 18, Orville took up one of the first passengers on a demonstration flight, and they crashed. Orville only broke his leg, but the passenger, Lieutenant Thomas Selfridge, died. He was the first airplane crash victim.

Wilbur was terribly upset when he heard the news, but after a few days, he was once again determined to prove that flight could be safe. Still in France, he went on more than 100 flights, many of them with passengers. On December 31, Wilbur flew in and won the French Commission of Aviation race, breaking all records with a flight of 2 hours, 20 minutes, 23.2 seconds and 77 miles (123.9 kilometers).

By the time of this 1909 photo, the Wright brothers were known across the world as pioneers of flight. This photo was taken by a French pilot named Leon Bollee.

Celebration

After Wilbur returned to Dayton, President William Howard Taft invited the brothers to the White House and presented them with medals. On June 17 and 18, 1909, the city of Dayton threw a big celebration for the brothers. On June 28, the final tests of the Army plane were a great success—Orville flew around the field just over 79 times. And on October 4, 1909, Wilbur flew over New York City during a celebration as a crowd of more than one million people watched in awe.

Across the Channel and into Wa

In 1909, the London newspaper *Daily Mail* offered a prize of 1,000 British pounds sterling, which was about 5,000 dollars at that time, to the first person to fly an airplane across the English Channel. That amount of money would be worth about $100,000 in today's money. Wilbur Wright decided not to do it, but others were ready to try. Among them was Louis Bleriot, a French pilot who had designed many **gliders** and airplanes. Bleriot decided to fly a **monoplane,** a design he preferred. In July 1909, Bleriot became the first man to fly across the Channel.

Once Europeans had seen Wilbur Wright's wing-warping system, they added it to their own planes and were able to fly farther and faster. In August 1909 in France, American engineer and pilot Glenn Curtiss won a race in which Bleriot was one of his fiercest competitors. Curtiss flew 12.4 miles (20 kilometers) at 46.5 miles (74.8 kilometers) an hour.

Louis Bleriot had an injured foot at the time of the flight contest, but he did not let that stop him from winning.

Flight safety

Countries began to hold contests and flying exhibitions, with pilots performing amazing flying stunts. Believe it or not, pilots and passengers at that time did not wear seat belts when they flew. Some tied themselves in with rope, but most did not. Over 30 people had died in airplane accidents by 1910.

When her plane hit **turbulence,** one popular American pilot, Harriet Quimby, and a passenger bounced out of their seats and fell to the ground. Both died. After that, flyers finally decided to start using seat belts and wearing helmets.

Airplanes in war

In 1911, Italy sent airplanes to Libya to do combat. By 1912, the French Army had a fleet of 254 airplanes. When World War I (WWI) started in 1914, countries around the world began to furiously design and manufacture airplanes. Each side knew it was in a race with the other, and that airplanes would play an important part in the war.

WWI pilots flew over enemy territory to observe movements and positions from the air. Machine guns became popular weapons to use from airplanes. By 1915, a Dutch engineer had figured out how to install machine guns in the airplane's nose, or front end. The guns would fire between the **propeller's** rotations so that they would not shoot holes into the propeller blades. Pilots used the machine guns to engage in mid-air fights at close range. Before the war ended in 1918, engineers had developed a way to drop bombs from devices on the planes.

A FLIGHT LESSON

Harriet Quimby was one of the first women pilots in the United States. She was also a writer for a magazine called *Leslie's Illustrated Weekly*. In 1911, she wrote an article for the magazine about learning to fly. In the article, she wrote the following about the feeling of flight:

"There is no exaggeration regarding the much-reported sense of fascination that accompanies a flight, however low, through the air. The feel of the first freedom experienced as the wheels leave the ground makes the student eager for a longer flight."

WWI bombers were more advanced than the Wright brothers' planes, but they were built based on similar design principles.

Wings over the World

World War I had forced airplane designers and manufacturers to develop the fastest, most powerful planes they could. Before the war, the fastest planes could fly up to 75 miles (121 kilometers) an hour and reach an **altitude** of about 10,000 feet (3,048 meters). By the end of the war in 1918, planes could fly about 120 miles (193 kilometers) an hour and reach altitudes of 20,000 feet (6,096 meters).

By this time, **ailerons** were replacing the wing-warping parts the Wright brothers had invented. Soon ailerons were being used on many airplanes. In 1915, the first plane made from metal flew, but it was slow. It took about fifteen years for engineers to develop a metal plane that flew as well as those made from wood, because the weight of the metal had to be taken into account.

Flying over the Atlantic

In 1919, a U.S. Navy *Curtiss NC-4* became the first airplane to fly across the Atlantic Ocean. Soon after that, **civilians** tried to fly across the Atlantic. None succeeded until June 14, 1919, when British flyers John Alcock and Arthur Brown flew from Newfoundland to Ireland in about 16 1/2 hours. In 1927, American Charles Lindbergh flew from New York to Paris in 33 1/2 hours, becoming the first man to fly alone nonstop across the Atlantic.

Charles Lindbergh stands proudly in front of the *Spirit of St. Louis*—the airplane that carried him safely across the Atlantic.

The progress of flight

In the 1920s, commercial airliners started carrying passengers. At first the planes were simple, but soon passengers were offered more comfortable seats and meals. In 1924, the first around-the-world plane trip took place. It took six months to fly the 27,553-mile (44,333-kilometer) trip.

The first regular air service carrying passengers flew between Paris, France, and Brussels, Belgium.

By the 1930s, many planes being made were **monoplanes.** Howard Hughes, an airplane pilot and manufacturer, flew a monoplane called the *Hughes Racer* across the United States in record-breaking time in 1937. The trip from California to New Jersey took only 7 hours and 28 minutes.

WOMEN TAKE TO THE AIR

Women were also making news as pilots. By 1911, about five women had pilot's licenses. In 1916, 25–year–old American Katherine Stinson toured England, China, and Japan in her airplane. In 1932, Amelia Earhart was the first woman to fly alone across the Atlantic Ocean. Amy Johnson, an English woman, was the first woman to fly from England to Australia.

Speed and Stealth

In 1929, a British flier named Frank Whittle got an idea to build a **turbojet** engine powered by the hot **exhaust** it produced. His fellow pilots thought he was crazy, and Britain's Air Ministry said it would not work. By 1939, though, a company with a contract from the British government to build a jet airplane asked Whittle to redesign the engine for them. In Germany, Hans von Ohain had a similar idea at almost the same time. By 1939, the turbojet engine had been put to use. By 1944, the German jet, called the *Me 262*, was flying up to 500 miles (805 kilometers) an hour. The British jet, the *Gloster Meteor*, also worked well, but it could not fly as fast.

Chuck Yeager is shown here with the plane in which he broke the sound barrier. The U.S. military kept Yeager's flight a secret for eight months because they did not want other countries to know they had a plane that could travel so fast.

The airplane and the jet fighter were valuable tools during World War II, which lasted from 1939 to 1945. The United States, Japan, and England built huge aircraft carriers so planes could take off and land in the sea. Planes flew hundreds of missions over enemy territory.

Breaking the sound barrier

Sound travels at about 700 miles (1,127 kilometers) an hour. Jet engines allowed airplanes to approach this great speed, but they would shake violently. When pilots doing experiments would fly that fast, their planes would sometimes break apart, and pilots were killed. Pilots began to call this point the **sound barrier.** Engineers decided to design a plane that could hold up under this kind of stress.

SUPER-POWERED JETS

By 1953, the United States had Air Force jets that could fly 864 miles (1,390 kilometers) an hour. By 1976, England and France's **supersonic** jet, the *Concorde,* was making regular flights. Some of the largest commercial jets flown today are called jumbo jets. One of the largest, the *Boeing 747,* can seat up to 524 passengers and fly for seventeen hours without stopping. Another, the *Airbus,* holds 555 passengers on two levels, and hauls mail and other cargo. The makers of the *Airbus* plan to include gyms and casinos on some planes.

An American manufacturer, Bell Aircraft Company, built the *X-1*—a plane that was sturdy and shaped like a bullet. Engineers were learning that the more **streamlined** a plane was, the better it could fly through the air. On October 14, 1947, Captain Chuck Yeager flew the *X-1* and successfully broke the sound barrier.

A turning point

The Wright brothers' contribution is almost too much to measure. As a result of their efforts, Orville lived to see airplanes fly at speeds beyond the speed of sound!

Since the flight at Kitty Hawk, airplanes have been used not only for war, but for bringing food and supplies to people who need them. Air travel allows family members to live far apart yet see one another regularly. Airplanes make everything faster, from mail delivery to personal travel. Patients are flown to hospitals by airplane or helicopter, and organs for transplants are flown to hospitals from state to state. Flight has changed the world in ways the Wright brothers never could have imagined.

The U.S. Air Force and Boeing have built the B-2 stealth bomber. This unusual-looking jet can carry both regular and nuclear bombs. The plane is unique because it is difficult to **detect** with **radar** and other detection systems.

Important Dates

1783		Montgolfier brothers invent hot-air balloons
1853		Cayley's **glider** sails across valley
1867	April 16	Wilbur Wright born
1871	August 19	Orville Wright born
1896		Otto Lilienthal dies while gliding; Wilbur Wright starts studying flight
1899		Wright brothers make plans to test gliders at Kitty Hawk
1900		Wright brothers go to Kitty Hawk for first flight experiments
1901		Wright brothers return to Kitty Hawk to do more experiments
1902		More flight experiments at Kitty Hawk
1903	December 17	Wright brothers make first powered flight at Kitty Hawk
1904	Spring	Wright brothers start flying *Flyer II* at Huffman's Prairie
1906		Santos-Dumont flies in France
1908	May	Wright brothers return to Kitty Hawk, fly in upright seats
	August 8	Wilbur Wright flies in France
	September 3	Orville Wright flies demonstration plane for U.S. Army
	September 18	Orville Wright crashes during demonstration flight, passenger is killed
1909	July	Louis Bleriot becomes first to fly over English Channel
1912	May 30	Wilbur Wright dies of an illness called typhoid fever
1914		Airplanes first used in World War I
1919		First plane, a *Curtiss NC-4*, flies across the Atlantic
1924		First around-the-world flight
1927		Charles Lindbergh becomes first man to fly alone across Atlantic
1932		Amelia Earhart is first woman to fly solo across Atlantic in the *Spirit of St. Louis*
1937		Howard Hughes makes record-breaking flight across United States in 7 hours, 28 minutes
1939		First jet plane is flown
1947		Chuck Yeager breaks **sound barrier**
1948	January 30	Orville Wright dies after having a heart attack

Glossary

abbey   building in which monks live

aileron   flap on airplane wing that allows the plane to bank and roll and give the pilot control over the aircraft

altitude   vertical height above the horizon of the earth

apprentice   someone who learns a skill or trade by working closely with those who already know the trade

bank   slope or incline of an airplane; planes bank when they make a turn

biplane   airplane that has two sets of wings, one on top of the other

camber   curve of the wings of an aircraft

catapult   device used to launch airplanes or other objects to flying speed

civilian   person not working for the military, police, or fire service

detect   find something out using specialized instruments

elevator   device on an airplane to help the pilot control upward and downward movement

exhaust   gas or moisture that escapes from an engine

glider   aircraft without an engine, powered only by air and a pilot

monk   person who has taken a religious vow and lives in a monastery

monoplane   airplane with one set of wings

propeller   fan-like blades on the front of an airplane that turn and help push the plane through the air

radar   electronic device that locates objects, such as airplanes, that usually cannot be seen with the eye; radar can tell the location and speed of airplanes

rudder   movable piece of metal at the rear of an airplane that steers the plane right or left

sound barrier   point near the speed of sound at which the pressure of the air pushing against the aircraft becomes so strong that it produces a shock wave and puts great stress on the aircraft

streamlined   designed to have a smooth surface and usually a long, slim shape so that when the object moves it has few surfaces to push against the air

supersonic   greater than the speed of sound in normal air temperature, which is about 767 miles (1,234 kilometers) per hour

turbojet   engine that compresses air and fuel, which is lit, creating gases that propel the aircraft

turbulence   in air travel, a disturbance in air motion; flying in air turbulence is like riding down a bumpy road

wingspan   distance from the tip of one wing to the tip of the other

Further Reading

Connolly, Sean. *Amelia Earhart*. Chicago: Heinemann Library, 2000.

Hewitt, Sally. *Air and Flight*. Danbury, Conn.: Children's Press, 2000.

Taylor, Michael J. H. *Chronology of Flight*. Broomall, Penn.: Chelsea House, 1999.

Index